Thoughts Of a Mature Mind

MARLO BROWNE

Copyright © 2022 Marlo Browne

All rights reserved. No part of this book is to be copied, recorded or otherwise transmitted without the prior, express, written consent of the author.

Passionate Words
Editing Services

(IG - @passionate.words.editing246)

Dedication

I want to acknowledge all of the poets who inspired me and gave me prompts to test my mind and encouraged me to write on new topics. I also want to thank all of my fans and supporters who have stuck with me as I travel along my poetic journey.

Contents

Dear Poet	7
Binary	12
Introspection	14
Changes	16
Victimized	19
A Plate Full Of Hearts	21
Wish	23
The Casual Observer	25
Inhumane	29
Arachnophobia	31
Untitled	33
The Covid Chronicles: Ashen Arc	35
I Am A Bajan	38
Thoughts Of A Mature Mind	40
Thoughts Of A Mature Mind: The Conversation	44
Dear Future Generation	48
Beauty	52
This Pen And Pad	54
A Stranger I Became	59

Universal	62
Too Tired	65
Untitled	67
Lyrically I Am	69
The Challenge	72
Venting V	74
Transitional	77
What We Can Truly Be	79
Stereotypical	82
On The Nights That We Don't Make Love	87
Write Me A Poem	90
I Hate You	93
Dear God	96
Mythical	100
Pariah	102
Wonderment	104
To Me	106
Time Will Tell	108
About The Author	111

Dear Poet

Dear poet,
If I could speak my truth
Then I would testify about three things
That aren't trending,
I am well versed,
Yet here I stand like a prosecutor
Presenting evidence incrementally for a plaintiff postulating that people
Are complicit in a conspiracy
Where human rights no longer exist.

Scenario 1:

From the first date of man
There was never a mandate stating that our bodies weren't ours,
Now they want to force us.
If I cite St. Vincent as a reference
Then tell me why they want to
Impede the development of young minds by threatening the jobs of teachers,
Subjugated to PCR tests
Where your reluctance to comply can affect your

livelihood.
Trypanophobia aside,
Psychogenic vasovagal syncope,
Febrile feelings and swelling of the deltoid region can occur,
Yet, still they want to force us,
Yet abortion is a choice,
Approximately 125 000 of these procedures are done daily on a global scale,
Yet this pales in comparison to the scope of the underlying problem
Women are subjected to misogyny
Virtually and physically harassed,
Yet there is no vaccine that can be
Injected into the deltoid muscle to reduce the risk of unwanted and
Unsolicited sexual approaches,
Even though the risk perception is high,
There is no vaccine to eliminate the risks that are concomitant
With predatorial attitudes that manifests into stalking and other forms of domestic abuse,
Still abortion is a choice,
So tell me,
If women have a choice to do what they want with their own bodies,
Why can't we?

I am a poet that can be pretty provocative,
Yet every time that this poet has spoken
I ensure that you understand that
These lyrics come from a place of deep thoughts.
Internally, I am rich with no limits,
Deliberately giving insight into mosaics,
So instead of being a bright spark,
I am a light beacon standing beside a blue lotus
illuminating a prosperous future where we could
Delve deeper into mental health issues so that we
could prevent events that constitute scenario 2...

Scenario 2:

Strained from stressors until he can't see a way out,
He places the cylinder of propane in the corner;
Determined that if this noose around his neck doesn't
do the deed that he requires,
Then it would be his due diligence to make sure that
his secondary attempt is successful.
So he stands in the chair,
Pulls the knot of the noose tighter,
Kicks the chair away so that he could be hanging,
His life essence disappears.
From April to early August 2021,
There was a steady increase in male suicide,

Which is indicative in the deterioration of male mental health –

Yet where are the outreach programs where we can reach out?

So castigated for our bad behavior

That sometimes they don't see the good,

So often perceived as emotionally unavailable

That they don't hear when we speak up or speak out,

So before the descriptive statistics escalate and you make more inferences,

I ask,

"Can you help us?"

Scenario 3:

I made mention of this earlier,

But allow my pen to make the connections like lines formed as you go from dot to dot:

She has been financially dependent,

Her options are scarce since

The resources have depleted with the surge of these Covid cases.

In a mood, he lashes out,

Now blood spouts from her head,

Yet he claims that he loves her;

Possessed by the mentality where he believes that he owns her.

He repeats this vicious cycle of break up, then make up, sexual abuse and manipulation
While he thinks that she isn't strong or determined enough to leave him,
Taking the vagina away because
You know,
'It belongs to him!'
Yet when she hesitates, his first question is
'Who else have you been having sex with?'
So when she finally has the courage to leave, he can't take it,
Using their children as props so that he could have an advantage,
Where did the time go?
Now he is the one crying,
Now he is the one hurting,
How can you act as if you are victimized
When you are the one who created the victim?

Binary

If this world was binary,
Then the wavelengths between these crests and troughs would make more sense to me.
Down in the valley,
We sometimes lose faith.
The external influences can warp our minds,
Pulling and pushing us like equal forces going in opposite directions.
We isolate,
Becoming socially distant even before it became a precedent for Covid.
This coping mechanism,
Although unhealthy, causes us not to lash out.
Instead we choose not to hurt others with words
Since their egress through loose lips could never be reversed.
Hurt,
Manifested by emotions evoked through egregious errors
Extrinsically motivated to make you vent,
Yet still we rise,
Phonetically silent like letters that are never pronounced,

So we hurry,
Expending energy as we climb hills,
Positivity perched, paunched with a protruding belly until it pops,
As we transition from depression to mania
We uplift, inspire and be inspired,
Until we attain some semblance of normalcy,
That middle ground,
That grey area that is between ying and yang
Showing us that the world could never be
Binary.

Introspection

Internally auditing my past actions
I take note of you,
Fond feelings forced out of my mind so that I can focus.
You are no longer a cog in my system
Theorizing that you are a crucial component that makes me-
Whole,
Holistic healing through therapeutic teachings makes
My recent reactions reflect the person that I am aiming to be,
Chronologically categorizing current events that would leave emotions in dents.
So, as I indent, like if I'm a new paragraph
It is no wonder that this chapter in the story of my life feels different;
Yet I still think of you.
An errant thought placed in a habitat where you had lived rent-free,
Now you have been evicted;
Yet, like a stubborn squatter, you linger,
Lying in wait like an apex predator

Hoping that I would slip up,
Injuring myself mentally since I would be stuck in a loop
That would be based on you,
I love me more though,
So as the emotions simmer,
I relax,
Slowly taking myself through
Introspection.

Changes

IInspired by the prompt 'A Perfect Day in my life would be'

A perfect day in my life would be:
Waking up in a world where
Bullies who belittled, beguiled and berated autistic and dyslexic children
Would pay penance for projecting their vast insecurities,
Psychological first aid wouldn't be needed for the mental injuries
Sustained by the traumatic experiences where they were perceived as retarded
Simply because the developmental process behind their thoughts was slower.
Stones wouldn't be thrown at them just because they were different
They would be loved and appreciated in a world where normal doesn't
Have an accurate definition;
That would be my first 6 hours.
My second 6 hours would consist of a world where women
In the Middle East weren't held captive by traditional

religious practices
Where breaking a dress code might mean certain death,
Yet women who wore hijabs are respected,
Not perceived as terrorists due to an inherent fear of the Taliban,
While women who lived in the west were paid more for their contributions
Since the world didn't see them as being subservient to men.
My third 6 hours would constitute:
A society where black men wouldn't be ostracized for showing emotions
Their problems would be discussed with their partners without the fear of sounding feminine
Those same black men wouldn't fear putting their hands in their pockets
Only to be shot dead by trigger happy officers who believed that they should
Shoot first and ask questions later,
So in my final 6 hours of my perfect day,
I would hope that poets could use their respective platforms to
Speak on social issues that bother us,
Push pens so that they could pass past fears so that we can break barriers
So that by 2022,

There would be more than one Brandon Leake or
Amanda Gorman
My perfect day would be one
Where poetry could change the world.

Victimized

Inspired by the prompt 'Diamond in the Dust'

Dancing with dichotomy,
Dueling detrimentally with a duality of character and images,
Imagery intact,
Yet makeup can't hide your inner bruises,
Smiling through salutations seemed to set the scene for serenity
Since you believed that you couldn't win.
Possessed by paranoia,
Poignant, even though he punched you;
He wanted to be in the right clique.
Yet this looked like a 'copy and paste' of the life that he has been through –
A diamond in the dust?
Even though he scratched the surface, it didn't stop your inner beauty from shining through,
Sculpted from scratch,
Hardened by possible permutations,
Surviving through sheer tenacity,
Even though you are a victim, you put on a brave

face for the world to see,

While he is unable to handle the attention that other men are giving you.

He looks innocent,

Yet he is insecure,

You have the aptitude and appropriate attitude to let down many men who approach you,

Yet he doesn't see this.

Even though you try to appease and ameliorate the conditions

That constitute the components of your relations,

Shipped to a billing address where you love him,

Still he doesn't see,

So he beats you to a pulp.

With your last ounce of strength,

You text,

'Can you help me please?'

A Plate Full Of Hearts

Inspired by the prompt 'A Plate Full of Hearts'

If I had a plate full of hearts
Then I would choose two that resonate with these treble clefs,
The melancholic music that accompanies a rhetoric that tries to convince me that
We are.....
Prone to maladaptive behaviors,
Prone to make errors since to err is to be human,
If I had to puncture those hearts,
Then as the blood flows,
It would lose its sanguine color,
Oxygen-deprived,
Which represents the look of tired mothers whose sons became
More uncouth through substance abuse,
Rebellious,
Mouthy,
Impressionable,

140/90,
The ratio of systolic to diastolic pressure escalates,
140/90,
Knock knock,
They hear the soft tap on the doors,
Knock knock,
Now they get up while the blood flows,
Knock knock,
As they open,
The police officers have warrants to inspect their homes,
140/90,
Now they look pale,
The officers search,
140/90,
The blood continues to flow,
The officers find cocaine,
140/90,
Now the blood flow stops,
The mothers collapse,
They could protect their sons no more,
Now the sons want to repent,
Yet it is too late,
Where did the hearts go?

Wish

In order to master peace
I wish that I could write a masterpiece,
Packed with pieces of positivity
Piercing and peering through the hearts of many,
So that I could change the course of conversation
Through the direct dissemination of information,
Allowing you to make a face similar to one where you sensed
A stimulus pungent enough to affect your olfactory organs
Which meant that these words have an intrinsic value.
I am in a mood,
So I can't,
I am afraid to write a story that my heart doesn't want to tell,
Where, as I visualize the impact of the impending collision
The sound of silence is synonymous to a recording where the audio cuts off,
As the distance between the vehicles lessens
I wonder what was your last thought,

I wonder what life lesson that you would have found applicable to this situation

Now they hit,

Smashed up,

Now you draw your last breath,

Flat-line.

The Casual Observer

Saturday was my birthday so she asked,
'What are you doing for it?'
Before my brain could formulate thoughts so my mouth could answer,
I noticed how the glasses fit on the brim of her nose,
I noticed how her eyebrow raised eager with anticipation for my swift response,
I noticed that as I turned a year older
I was more than able to differentiate between someone being physically attractive and
Someone being beautiful,
So what I seek is a beauty that is subcutaneous,
What I seek is the truth told so eloquently that it could be heard
Even though it had been said smoothly, sweetly and softly like a murmur.
So I responded,
'Nothing! I have to work today,'
Startled, she posed some more questions like
'What about after?'
'What are you drinking?'
'Don't you have fun?'

Yet, what caught my attention was when she told me to live.

Live?

What does that mean?

Overthinking had been my forte

Yet, now I choose to listen,

Live,

Irrespective of current conditions

I thought about how that four letter word means something different to so many different people,

Live,

Still I remain a casual observer, unable to understand the intricacies of human behavior,

Unable to breathe

Like if I am the victim of a spontaneous pneumothorax

Where the air circulating around my lungs seems toxic,

Live in a place where spontaneity defies the concept of a logical trajectory,

Live so that you can make memories

By gaining and garnering experience through the making of mistakes,

Be prepared to fail,

Live,

Not affected by societal pressures where we are pressed to conform

To norms and values that we don't believe in,
Live accordingly.
Still I remain a casual observer,
On the fence, hoping to weave through the traffic of misinformation
Listening-
To see if I could learn anything of significance,
Waiting-
To see if I'm lackadaisical or indecisive,
While the onlookers look on to see if I'm like Benjamin Sisko
Trekking through uncharted territory so that I could reveal the star that I am becoming,
Waiting-
To see if people care about themselves enough to follow protocols,
Waiting-
To see if we would no longer have curfews
Waiting-
To see if future plans make sense since what is being tested is my resilience,
Waiting-
To see if they would leave me alone,
I'm a canvas that they want to paint their story on,
Pacing-
Since I can't stay still,

Pacing,
Thinking,
Then I stopped,
Since I have found the beauty in me.

Inhumane

If I had to write about myself
Then I would tell you that
I'm someone who likes to provoke thoughts and have deep conversations,
Yet I'm more than that,
I grew up in an area where men would beat each other with machetes
Then speak to each other later,
A 'bust head' was frequent,
Yet they often forgot what the argument was about
I grew up in an era where-
The phrase 'we outside' sometimes meant playing dominoes under a street light
Wooden tables were constructed for this sole purpose, while music blasted on boom boxes
We spoke well but we were accustomed to ghetto living,
I reminisce about eating biscuits and sardines every time I hear Big Poppa's 'Juicy',
Cherished our dear mothers even before Tupac wrote 'Dear Mama',
I heard gangsters rap
Yet, does that make me a gangster?

I wanted to be big,

Now I'm 'Notorious' for casually decimating every avaricious attempt

Used by upper echelons to belittle unfortunate members of society

While figuring out how to grieve,

A journey made without a gurney,

Pensive with a pinch of quiet,

So, that every time my pen speaks, my words plunge to abysmal depths,

Yet I never want to write about death

So that every time I see August 11th, I remember you,

Burned beyond recognition while being trapped in a car trunk

Yet, almost 6 years later and still there is no better outcome

Another black man who is dead before 30,

Now Columbus, Ohio seems like a red flag to me

'If there's any justice in the world,'

Like Lemar sang about in 2004,

Then no stone would be left unturned until my childhood friend got the justice that he deserved

Yet there is nothing,

Crickets chirping, as I think

How can humans be so inhumane?

Arachnophobia

If I had shown my heart less
Would that make you heartless?
Arachnophobia
So I avoided your long legs
While you lingered, licking lips lasciviously
As you try to tempt
Me,
Sultry like a siren speaking a sonnet
You try to lure me,
Like a lost little fly entering your carefully spun web,
You hoped to devour
Me,
Yet I refused to yield to temptation,
A proud pilgrim proceeding to progress, passing every past test
Through perseverance rather than pilferage,
So even if I tried to sneak a peek
My inner peace would suffice,
Never Adam
Yet I wanted to taste that forbidden fruit thrice,
A battle between heart and mind where Lucifer asked

'What is your greatest desire?'
So even though I wanted to say, 'You,'
I chose to live
While he expired
Ad infinitum.
P.S I almost gave in...

Untitled

Like a young Shirley Jones in her prime, she asks,
'Who can I run to?'

And I had no response.

She needed a safe space where she could unwind through trying times

While she aged like a glass of fine red wine,

Instead I was emotionally invested in life enough to dissect it,

So I had no response

Since the muse I see was like music that moved insurmountable mountains of nerves

So that the fiery feelings that were residual, created passionate moments

Where momentum had to be slowed

Until it reached a point of inertia illustrating a taciturn turn of events,

So when she asked,

'Who can I run to?'

I thought about what I was running from

While she imagined a big burly man that could press her head against his chest

While she sighed in relief, forgetting all of her problems

For in that moment, he was the solution

An ideal image of strength that had been projected in her mind quite often

So, as that movie continued to play out,

I slowly realized that I wasn't that guy.

The Covid Chronicles: Ashen Arc

Triggered by the sound of a trigger,
I watch,
As events unfold and the truth is revealed
I traverse my memories until I reach the point where the world was in a frenzy,
It was June 2020 where George Floyd represented a stereotypical segment of history,
Immaculately illustrated to the point where people protested in the midst of a pandemic,
'We have had enough!' –
Or so we thought.
Fast forward to April 2021 where Daunte Wright wasn't done right,
Shot,
Now his life was gone in a flash,
With no yellow lightning or a force of speed to reverse time to bring him back
Two separate murders occurring in the same state,
Two different incidents, yet the cops got the same charges-
Murder of the 2nd degree.

Are we really surprised to see a drawn out trial questioning integrity
Even though a murder was committed in front of our eyes?
Are we really surprised that a 'use of force' expert would say
That Chauvin was completely justified in his pinning technique
Even though for months you chanted,
'I can't breathe?'
A foot on the neck is wrong, right?
Pause there for a second,
In fact, let's go back to April 2020 where a black young man was killed
In Barbados by a police officer,
Not a white one, but by a black one who placed his foot on the guy's neck
So for a whole year, a mother got no justice
For a whole year, that mother mourned while a lot of us were distracted
Black lives matter, right?
Tell me...
Why is it that a lot of you go silent when blacks kill their own?
How many of us black men have to die before we can become statistically significant?
Black men are kings?

Yet if we wear our hair naturally, we are criticized by black women

As if hair growth is directly proportional to job performance,

Black men are loved, right?

So why do we hear black women say that they want no 'broke nigga'

If money and status are temporary, then tell me why we are judged by such superficial means

Yet we puff our chest and say loudly-

'BLACK LIVES MATTER!!!'

So tell me which ones?

If you all believe that we are all treated equally,

Then I guess that this arc of ash

Isn't the only thing affecting your visibility.

I Am A Bajan

If I told you that I was a Bajan,
Then that might confuse you.
I am a Black man,
Yet I bleed gold and ultramarine.
Breaking our colonial bonds,
We would charter into new territories as we become a republic,
Only 166 square miles, yet our literacy rates extend beyond 95%
You see,
When you talk about Barbados,
You might think about Rihanna,
Yet our culture is deeper,
From devouring delicious delicacies such as flying fish and cou cou
To every other day, you could savor a 'bread and two',
Or you could wait for Saturdays for pudding and souse,
You see, being a Bajan, or Barbadian, to me means that you can remember
Dalton Sinclair Bishop, otherwise known as Jackie Opel,

So every time you 'get down on your knees and cry me a river', remember spouge,
'Telling me to forget that my navel string was buried right here so'
As I switch from the Queen's English to dialect,
Perusing the words of Dr. Anthony 'Gabby' Carter, as I traverse through Emerton,
If you take Covid away,
Then we would showcase cultural diversity,
On the first Monday of August,
The voices in my head would want me to wuk up behind a bevy of beauties,
While the gals roll it, asking me, 'wha gine on?'
Glass of Mount Gay rum in hand-
'Chipping down the road with me own woman'
Not always knowing the name, yet 'I know the face',
This is Grand Kadooment, where feathery costumes are plenty and
The women are 'too sweet when I wine pon them'
Yet I digress,
My country has been depicted as a paradise
Where you can frolic on beautiful white sand and amazing blue beaches,
Our people are hospitable,
This is why I will never trade being
A Bajan.

Thoughts Of A Mature Mind

If I said that I love you

Then how can I not love all of you?

Period pains paralyze and prevent you from performing your normal activities

While hematuria, dysuria and urination frequency makes you conscious of self,

Unable to trust,

Endometriosis makes you a skeptic,

You don't want to be pitied,

Hunched over, hoping that no one would see you struggle to ascend the stairs,

Yet, there it comes,

The frantic concern as a voice asks

'Are you ok?'

Though polite, that provokes you,

Initially you say no,

Yet Paracetamol could only do so much,

Then it comes,

The blood flows down your legs until it becomes ubiquitous,

Embarrassed, you could say nothing,
So he rushes to help,
You direct him to your bag
So that you can change the tampon,
Yet it hurts,
That excruciating feeling that you could bear no more,
Supervisor notified,
You winced,
He returns with your bag,
They escort you to the bathroom,
It hurts,
In a small voice, you say,
'Get my husband!'
As I reveal the thoughts of a mature mind
Allow me to assure you that this dynamic duo will get through this,
Awareness improved,
So although the dysmenorrhea intensifies even before I arrive,
We will get through this,
Yet you worry,
I wanted another kid,
So I mistook your pain for pleasure,
Now you see me
While I see you,

Broken,
Emotionally damaged,
How was I going to react?
Would I be supportive?
These thoughts plagued your mind,
Afraid of confrontation, you watch me,
What will I say?
What will be my first words?
Yet, that wasn't me,
Instead of being inconsiderate, I considered our next move,
So I said,
'It's going to be ok.'
I love you,
Spoken words of reassurance that extirpate fickle feelings of fear
Felt instead of foraging the flora found around us,
You are…
The flower that possesses pulchritudinous petals that only opens up with poise,
Your vulnerability is a sequestered spot
Never to be exploited,
Instead it is a rare commodity that is seen by the most trustworthy,
You are…
The epitome of elocution,

So how could I not love you?

Partners paired perfectly like peanut butter and jelly,

Now we make our way home, turning your mishap into conversation,

Bonding together strongly like covalent bonds in chemistry,

I love you,

Caressing you carefully so that you know that you could put your trust in me,

If we are partners,

Then how can I not want to know about your medical history

Yet I want our genitalia to exchange salutations?

We are the ultimate union

So our actions are manifested through these thoughts of mature minds.

Thoughts Of A Mature Mind: The Conversation

She said,

I feel like less of a woman,
This laparoscopic salpingectomy
Made me cancel our dreams,
Our son is 7 years old and
Thoughts of another child seemed
To exist in a different lifetime,
You said that you love me, but do you really?
My chronic pelvic pain posed a problem
Where we had to slow down every time
We gyrated hips,
We had to keep it down to ensure that
The neighbors did not know how to recall
Our perfect passionate positions,
Now we pause,
My incisions itch,
My incisions hurt and I'm tempted
To scratch,
What will become of us?

I see her watching you,
The tantalizing temptation that tries
To turn you away from me,
She is the Delilah to my Sampson,
So if you value the hair on your head,
Then ignore her since you are unevenly yoked,
We have work to do,
So tell me, will you stand the test of time?
Or will you cower in the corner,
Clinging to crevices created through
Crossword clues?
You say that you want me,
Yet you push me away,
You say that you are in love with me,
Yet she flirts frequently with you,
I just can't cope with your indecision
So, are you going to show me
The thoughts of a mature mind
Or will you leave me guessing?

Theyoungandgifted:

If loving you was a losing game,
Then I would shuffle the deck of cards
While I sweetly seduce Lady Luck
So that I can get the hand that could

Bring us back to each other,
You are....
An ace of diamonds linking hearts together
As we traverse through this house of clubs,
We....
Are live, taking snapshots as we pass words
Going past this book of faces,
I try not to twitch, turning off televisions
While I show you that I am more
Than a social media presence,
You question my mature mind,
Yet I put aside prior personal preferences
To protect your pelvis
During your pelvic floor dysfunction.
I love you,
So if I wanted another kid,
We can adopt instead of trying to
Coax you into cold, cruel and careless copulation,
Creating an environment where you are....
Capricious,
I asked God for a partner and he sent you,
So I sought wisdom like Solomon
While I tried to conquer these sands
Of time,
An hourglass of emotions,
So, as they continue to slip through,

We move together in unison,
Soul-tied,
Ending this conversation that stemmed
From the thoughts of a mature mind.

Dear Future Generation

Inspired by the prompt 'The World We/You will Leave Behind'

Dear future generation

We messed up,

In this book of life, we often cut the pages that contain crude content

Replacing archaic qualities like kindness and empathy with a lack of manners and vanity,

You see,

Love no longer has a common scent,

Instead, it is a spiked drink composed of mendacity, manipulation and lust

So that when that intoxication disappears, you feel lovelorn,

Used, then thrown aside, like a stuffed animal that no longer comforts you when you are scared,

I used to wish that I would meet no more broken people,

Then I realized,

We are all broken, with no instruction manual passed down from prior generations

On how to fix the errors of our past ways,
We treat manners and decency with an air of skepticism
Since we fear that these are shown as the surface that hides an ulterior motive,
Humility is an acquired skill, attained by experience
So tell me, when will we celebrate life, instead of accomplishments?
We value things and use people
Yet, when they die, we cry, since we no longer have those human resources
Is it really that, or are we too afraid to express what we really feel?
We are all actors on different stages
So when the masks fall off
What lies beneath, like a stripped version of a beautiful song, are
The cracked fragments, when placed together, that form humanity.
Dear future generation
We messed up,
I am a young, Black man who has seen hurt,
So, in the following years which constitute my life's expectancy, allow me to be different,
You see, in the first 8 months of 2020, approximately 164 of us were gunned down,
Still, they don't say our names

Since that U-S doesn't feel as if we are a part of the United States,

One hundred and sixty four Black mothers cried, and those that did not, worried

Worried that their son or daughter may be next,

They are either pulled over, subjected to incorrect search warrants or

Just perceived as dangerous,

Yet that is only one side of the coin,

What about the other side where we kill ourselves?

We speak of unity, yet we flaunt our privileges over the heads of the less fortunate

We speak of unity, yet we exist separately,

I have seen some of us cry over life's tribulations,

Tormented by financial instability and the inability to provide for our families,

Evicted, we become insomniacs

Kings, struggling to find proper queens,

So tell me, future generation,

Will you listen to us?

Dear future generation

Let me talk to you for a second,

Seventy six years after the world warred with itself, here we go again

However, instead of using guns and atomic bombs, we fight over a needle,

Segregated into two groups:

Vaccinated vs unvaccinated, where the latter category is treated like lepers,

Stigmatized, so that when they get sick,

The basic human right of healthcare shouldn't be afforded to them,

If evolution is defined as the change in characteristics of a species over time,

Then specify the timeframe where we got so petty in our thinking,

These people, who are still our brothers and sisters, now fight alone,

So that when one of them dies, the main highlight is their unvaccinated state,

Reputations tarnished,

Jobs threatened, where sometimes even the chance of an interview is diminished,

So tell me future generation,

How will you improve on the world that we will leave behind?

Beauty

If I could paint my lyrics on your canvas
Then the world would know of your beauty.
These pen strokes would do more
Than highlight your countenances,
Instead they would create vivid images
That would showcase your vivacious personality,
Voluptuous,
So as I pay close attention to your hips,
Grant me the opportunity to
Introduce them to your thickness,
Mature mindset,
So I stand apart in a world that is prolific in body shaming,
Set by societal standards
The definition of beauty hinges
On a flawed physical construct,
Perfection is the sum of the absence of blemishes,
While emotional scars remain
Hidden behind the curtains of pretense,
We are presented with images of
Curvaceous creatures that sometimes lack good conduct,

While 'plus-sized' good women are overlooked,
Thrown aside because our friends can't see us next to them,
We crave the opinions of others
Rather than care about our own feelings,
We gloss over 'walking trophies' rather than try to create
An emotional connection,
Not me though,
I would rather consume soul food
Than try to break my teeth over eye candy,
So as I sculpt you, my 'La Pieta'
Then this work of art would denote your compassion,
It would represent a modern Madonna's
Maternal love for a son who died so that we could live,
So as I end,
Just remember that my pen David
Could slay any Goliath task,
So, as I present these two famous pieces,
Call me a polymath,
Call me the 21st century Renaissance man,
While I finished painting my lyrics on your canvas
As a melanated Michelangelo with a pen.

This Pen And Pad

Trigger warning: In this piece, I speak about autism, domestic abuse, rape and suicide.

With this pen and pad
I overcome the barriers associated
With verbal and written communication,
As I relive the memories of my childhood
I remember when they tried to stifle
The voice of an autistic singer,
Singing 'Suddenly' by Billie Ocean seemed to annoy them,
So they threw stones,
We tread through waters of ignorance,
Hoping for paradigm shifts,
Yet they spewed the same rhetoric
Too ignorant to differentiate between
A mental health illness and a developmental disorder,
So they call an autistic individual retarded,
Judging him because he talked different,
Laughing because he had a huge backpack,
While his brother and sister tried to stop the

bullying,
He cried, wondering what he did wrong,
An altruistic person, hoping that
His kindness would be reciprocated,
Yet it wasn't,
Even on his dark days, he still 'shined on yesterday',
Now, years later, as he won awards and
He was booked to sing at weddings, they praised him,
Still he loved them,
A stigma surrounds those who have special needs,
Yet little research is done
While misinformation becomes the latest currency,
So I ask,
Should they seek forgiveness
Or should he turn the other cheek?
With this pen and pad,
I would write another version of 'I'm Sorry',
Where police officers who ignored complaints from survivors
Of domestic abuse are reprimanded,
So even though his fragrance loiters on her skin,
You still say that it is consensual,
Instead of helping, you tell her to lie down,
Spread her legs and take it since that is her man,
You say this while your cerebral cortices

Lack the cognitive capacity to realize
That she is emotionally triggered when
You speak specific sentences,
Your emotional quotient is non-existent,
So although you see the signs, you ignore them,
Reticent,
Complicit even though you were not in the vicinity,
You ignored her,
Assigned with the task where you should 'protect and serve'
You couldn't reassure her that she would be fine,
Instead you laugh, even though her face was black and blue,
Her lips were a sanguine color,
She was the image of 'battered and abused',
Yet you ignored her,
A gesture made by a jester who didn't
Have the foresight to see the repercussions of his actions
Since he wanted to fit in,
He wanted to be a part of an informal organization where
He could be in control,
But at whose expense?
The expensive cost of her pain
Wasn't equivalent to his sense of humor,

So, on that dark night, he became the joker,
A career about to be ruined
As his negligence resulted in another life not being saved.
With this pen and pad,
My ink bleeds for troubled teens
Who are having suicidal thoughts,
Daily doses of negativity were doused
On their mental canvases,
Deaths escalated daily,
So they became psychologically scarred,
Stuck behind computer screens
They lived in a time that wasn't conducive
To their social wellbeing,
Online etiquette not taught or observed,
So how do you expect them to learn?
They can no longer touch,
Yet they yearn for that social interaction,
Isolation became the bane of their existence,
Which came as a result of the transition
From face to face learning
To a place where they are exposed
To pornographic images even though
They are supposed to be learning,
The teachers are stressed,
Torn between the traditional environment

And one where they feel more relaxed
Now the teens suffer,
They have no coping mechanism,
We forgot that a part of what makes
Learning enjoyable is the development
Of friendships that we form along the way,
So as I write on these topics and some
Of you may be triggered,
Just remember that I would rather
Ask for forgiveness than permission, so please, forgive me.

A Stranger I Became

A stranger I became,
These are woven words from a web
Of truth that serve as a testimony to
The travesties and tragedies that
I have been through and emerged from,
I was helpless,
Transported to a time where I saw
A little boy trodding with twitches of Tourette syndrome,
I stayed silent, full of dreams and aspirations,
Yet I was confused,
Since, although we have become
More scientifically enlightened and
Technologically advanced,
Still there is no procedure
That can correct neurological disorders,
His mother -
A slim silhouette smiling sheepishly
As the stigma tries to swallow her - spoke to me,
'What's wrong?'
I could say nothing,
Thinking thoughts as I tireless tried

To find an equation to balance this problem,
Yet it wasn't a problem,
It was his life,
Still he trodded on, without a worry
His face was the epitome of endurance
Still I could say nothing,
The thin line between sympathy and empathy seemed blurry,
My size 13 feet couldn't fit in his shoes' soles,
Then he looked at me, noting my apprehension
So he said,
'Don't worry, I'll be alright.'
In that moment, I understood what it meant to be truly alive.
A stranger I became,
I held your attention captive,
Yet my physical presence was in
A different geographical location,
Your ears are tuned in to the frequency
Of vibrations that travel from my mouth
Through the air until it tickles the tragi
On your exterior ear canal,
These words make the hair follicles on your legs stand up,
So I miss you, even though I never touched your skin,

Instead I touched your hearts,
You were the catalyst that alters
The rate of an exothermic reaction,
So as this heat is released and transferred between us,
I told you stories that made you
Think twice about whether or not
This pandemic was caused by
Coronavirus disease or depression,
You see, how is it that someone could
Love to go to work, rather than being at home?
How is it that we see someone
Deteriorating before our very eyes, yet we can say nothing?
We deflect, arguing about which striker
Sent a goalkeeper the wrong way
Yet the penalty for keeping our feelings in, is a detriment,
Yet you stay,
Ears pricked, eager to receive your next fix,
So although I became a stranger,
I dedicate this to you-
My poetic audience.

Universal

Inspired by the prompt 'Color Me Happy' by Kheneil Black

If you wanted to color me happy,
Then remove the mindset where my skin is associated with its absence,
Disassociate it from the pungent smell of evil,
Re-calibrate your thoughts so that we wouldn't be seen as illiterate and shaking spears,
Instead we wage war with words while taking care of their wards,
So tell me, how can the greatest poet of all time be William Shakespeare?
Google the highest paid writer and you will never see an image of melanin,
Yet, if white is an absent color, why is it packed with perks and privileges?
We learn of Bell, Edison and Tesla,
Yet we never knew of Latimer, Morgan, Woods, Washington or Walker,
They were lauders for being pioneers of medicine,
Yet they never issued a formal apology to Henrietta
Since they lacked the cells to propel their agenda,
We talk of reparations,

However, they never paid us for Tuskegee
Black men were subjected to unethical experiments,
Yet they are still perceived as dangerous to this day,
A death sentence, where even our opinions aren't the subject or the predicate
Pray for us,
Even when we fight for independence,
Poverty ensues,
Ghana and Haiti were the first Black nations to achieve this feat,
Yet what happened?
They suffered,
Put in a position where the world now scorns them,
Once full of riches,
Now nothing,
Haiti is despised worse than the serpent who was forced to crawl on its belly,
Its people are stigmatized, where people have said that they are nasty,
Yet, who is going to say sorry for the vile things that were done in the name of Christianity?
We cry,
We hurt,
Yet we compete, instead of co-operate,
So, instead of coloring me happy,
Grant me the opportunity to go into predominately white spaces,

Give me the chance to speak to them sternly and sincerely,

Allow my poetry to pull people together without being the two major sporting events,

Then maybe, just maybe,

These words and this message would become Universal.

Too Tired

I had a heartache,
It was the second night that I fell asleep,
Yet she understood,
My departure had left her in a bereft state,
While my body was burdened with an
Impending tension since I had not
Fulfilled my physiological needs,
She was my black beauty and as
Our delicate future hung in the balance,
I loathed the fact that I was too tired,
So I set my scope down while I set sights
On the battlefield,
I attended to my call of duty
While others acted like if
They had vision, but they were too blind to see
I had been a soft square and
She had been my final fantasy,
My heart had been a kingdom and
She held the keyblade to unlock it,
So we triggered chronometry and crossed
Into our destinies,
We are an amalgamation that attracted attention

Through our anomalous articulations,
Ambiguous, we anointed others with words
That left them ambivalent,
We birthed beautiful blessings
That were carefully constructed with candid cadence,
Determined and destined to escape
The impending levels of toxicity,
We lather our skins with daily affirmations.

Untitled

As you listen to three minutes
Of intensive wordplay, you fall for me,
Like heavy torrential rainfall on pavements
You fall for me,
My DM was the aperture for
Open and honest communication and
Through that, we hoped to cross
An ocean to be together,
So where do we start?
The road to love was long and difficult,
Our piqued curiosity caused us not to
Peep through avenues where
Our exes lingered, licking lips lustfully
While hoping that we aren't lucid enough
To recognize the realm of reality
Where we left them,
They were the caricatures of our past selves,
Now, as we swerve left, avoiding the cul-de-sac,
We are tempted to touch,
Closing the proximity so that we could be skin to skin,
Our morals felt fragile like a flower's petal

Falling gracefully as the seasons change
From spring to autumn and we are...
Tempted to fornicate,
Yet we wait,
Beneath the burden of the world's gaze
While we try not to buckle
Under the pressure of the expectations set upon us,
We wait,
Even though the cardinal sin of lust is at its peak,
I show remorse because I did not mean to make you fall in love
With me.

Lyrically I Am

Daintily dripping like a dew drop while
Delivering a powerful poetic prompt
She is beautiful,
Yet she didn't know it,
Before, she used to bewitch and beguile
Many men by making modern medicine
Through muscle memory,
An apothecary,
So, as you yearned for your weekly fix,
She was the succubus slowly sucking
Out your life's essence,
While she surreptitiously solicited
Another sorry sycophant sitting down,
Deep in despair, he looked up
At the gray skies,
He was trapped in her words,
She was his poetic seductress
So her tricky traits were a treat to him,
Toxicity elevated,
He picked a poison that he was too poor
To pursue,
A whiz kid,

He wanted to be in her essence,
A drunkard, still dumb enough to drink
More than he could handle
Then I came along,
Different, so she changed character
She asked,
'Who are you?'
Lyrically I am Gabriel Belmont
Traveling to Transylvania to defy death
To defeat a deadly Dracula who was
Drenched in blood,
I am never anxious,
So although I face many foes
I found a friend in my solitude,
My words became my vampire hunter and
Like a Lycan, my bite became the bane
To their kind,
I taste victory on this Hallows' Eve,
Scary sights no longer sleep here,
Instead, you are blessed with a bundle
Of talent that tantalizes through
Emblazoned moments,
I make eyes pop out
Without you eating spinach,
Got it?
Popeye eating spinach, moves

Mountains that were once mole-hills,
My mission?
To make every part of the globe know
About my talent,
So that when they hear Barbados
They don't think about our small size
Of 166 square miles or our lovely beaches,
Instead, they take note of the talent,
The hard work and dedication,
They notice how a life can change
With even the smallest ounce of opportunity
So the next time you ask,
'Who are you?'
Lyrically I am your equal.

The Challenge

I want you,
Yet the thoughts of my past insecurities
Scare me,
These are no longer memories eclipsed
By emotions,
Instead,
This was an exclusive entanglement
Between my heart and mind,
My mind meanders through Mozart's
Musical melodies where your voice was
Pitched perfectly with a harmony
That was never haphazard,
Silence isn't my favorite sound,
Instead, it was your voice calling my name,
My heart beats rhythmically to
The rhapsody of your tone,
So I wasn't tone deaf,
I was touched by the crotchets and
The treble clefs while you teased me
With songs from A to G minor,
Reach for me,
Touch my zenith with both hands

While we try to be as successful
As the Byzantine empire,
Hoping that it doesn't collapse,
Guarded from prior traumas hanging
Over my head like thieves slinking
From the shadows,
You now see my naked heart,
A combination of talent mixed together
Like granite with mortar and pestle,
We merge, as I become
The gift to your chemistry.

Venting V

It sickens me to my stomach
How is that we are human
Yet treated insignificantly like insects?
The ratio of new cases
Of coronavirus disease to deaths looks
Like an outlandish test cricket score but
Who is keeping the score on our mental health?
Three hundred for two,
Now if the West Indies cricket team had made that,
I would be jumping with jubilation but
Like them, we despise and detest defeat,
We dip into despair as we dabble in dirges
While we are dissenters
To the normalcy of the country's dissonance,
We no longer have an abundant harvest
Of happiness,
You took away our smiles,
How is it that you can raise the price
Of utilities, but cut our wages?
I feel scarred,
Looking down on these lying kings
While they are caught in your stampede

Of deceit,
R.I.P to you Mufasas,
Picture me singing like Peabo Bryson because
This whole new world has me changing my demeanour,
Even if shadows burn, music wouldn't be
As symbolic as James Ingram singing
The theme song from Sarafena,
Yet we prostitute ourselves,
Hoping that instead of being repulsive,
They stick their money
Into our economic slots and when
They pull out, we give birth to tourism,
A dearth of transparency was concomitant
With a bunch of hypocrites in healthcare
Swearing an oath to Hippocrates,
We....
Miss the ambiance of carnival while
Gyrating on big booties while
We.....
Sip on classic Caribbean rum,
Punching through pockets of innate tension,
We lower our guards,
Hoping for fruitful and friendly conversation,
Take me back to the days where
We were truly living and it wasn't

The government who caused us
To be truly suffering.

Transitional

I came in as Marlo,
Then I grew to be 'Young and Gifted',
I stepped away from shyness,
While I sobbed in silence when I set my short-term goals,
Feeding focus, I forgot to frolic while filtering my 'friends' list as I
Removed each goal from the checklist as I accomplished it,
I compiled my second book while I was grieving,
Night after night,
I asked God why I had to lose another friend in a summer month,
Still I wrote, escaping my cocoon of nervousness
While I peeled pieces of myself off so that you can peep through the partitions
To see my personality.
Personally, I chose to protect my peace
Since the hardest composition to create is an autobiography.
An ambivert, yet I swipe left of the spectrum as I enjoy being introverted,
Yet you see me, humble and talented, as I embrace the

dawn of a new year,

Now, here I am in the terminal, waiting on a bus to get home,

My achievements for the past year, though enjoyed, were still not celebrated,

I grew, I made professional and personal relationships,

Still I saw the world's problems,

Homeless women were becoming more prevalent and

As we go in and out of lockdown,

They were more susceptible to verbal, emotional and sexual abuse,

So that they could try to navigate and improve their situation,

I saw a boy sing loudly to himself, while adults wanted him to be quiet

Without trying to understand that this was his coping mechanism,

Now I board the bus, amidst the chaos and calamity

Congratulating myself, as I try to be a better person.

What We Can Truly Be

Pensive,

So I tried to proceed past prior prohibitions

That had me pondering possible permutations

Where I made you unhappy,

My attitude had changed towards certain things and

The stench of my happiness affected

Overworked olfactory organs of overprotective onlookers

Who can't control their contrition.

Since we can no longer be together,

Their miserable mumblings seem miserly,

They are curious,

So they concoct scenarios to cause confusion between them.

I love her,

Yet I struggle with the transition made

From being a single to committed man,

She loves him,

Yet she is worried since I am

Tethered to my constant filial obligations,
She blesses me like a beatitude
While my feelings towards this vicissitude
Almost make me push her away,
She hates this tug-of-war,
This push-pull mechanism made her doubt
That the load that I bear was worth her effort,
So there I stood,
Among the onlookers who believed
That we were destined to fail,
So that they could critique our attempts
To be a couple,
They wanted a discussion,
Yet I didn't want to give it to them,
So they lived vicariously through me,
Stalking my statuses and Instagram stories,
Even though they claim to hate me in public,
Secretly they watch me,
While I try to learn her love language,
I was not accustomed to her genuine and giving personality,
Yet she constantly gave me words of affirmation
Although that constant reassurance was draining,
I made her self-conscious,
I damaged her to her core,
Yet she still wants to stay with me,

Secure,
Safe,
She told me to let her love me and
As I am transported to 2004
When Mario wrote those lyrics,
I look past her anatomy and think of
The couple that we can truly be.

Stereotypical

She said,

'If you are truly a writer,
Then write me a story with words
That are more meaningful to me
Than my reality,
Let your consonants cater
To my creative consternations
While they caress me as they combine
With vowels to create cute compositions
That leave me..
Enthused and enchanted by the energy
That you exude when you speak to me,
I feel hurt sometimes,
Yet this hypomanic episode keeps me..
Going and going,
Not like the Energizer bunny but
I push past plateaus of paranoia
So that people are unable to perceive
My psychosis,
Still I feel hurt,
I dance with depression,

Daunted by debts that leave me debilitated,
I dive into the depths of despair,
Defined by a defeatist's declaration,
They don't understand,
They push, surprised that my mood swings
Back and forth,
Now I am your pendulum
Since you know the frequency of my oscillations,
To the average person, they may think
That I am moody,
Yet you know that this isn't stereotypical,
I have bipolar II disorder.'

He said,

'If you are an artist,
Then create a canvas where
My solitude can find solace in slumber,
Be the Van Gogh painting my starry night
So that I can have a sense of belonging,
Placate the poor,
Portray their petitions with each brushstroke,
While placing potato eaters amongst the upper echelons,
Illustrating that there is beauty in the struggle,
Allow me to reminisce about Rembrandt's

Return of the prodigal son
As I try to regain my place in civilization,
I thought that I was selectively social,
Yet my antisocial personality disorder
Causes me to treat those that I love
With a callous indifference,
Change my mindset while I digress
From the fact that I care nothing
About their feelings,
I need help,
I tried to find love,
Yet my past endeavors taught me
That they were incapable of showing it,
Those Mona Lisas could never capture my heart,
While you became the Da Vinci
Painting the portrait of my life
While increasing awareness of the disorder
That affects my social wellbeing.

It said,

'If you are a poet,
Then scribe me a stanza where
You found me a family where I haven't created victims,
You can be my Etheridge Knight,

Dying on the call of duty from a shrapnel wound,
Yet resurrected from the sweet smell
Of my perfume,
Narcotics could be your comfort
Catapulting you to instant success
As you put together pieces of poems
That take you away from the prison
Of your mind,
You can't escape me,
I have ripped families apart,
Leaving the tattered pieces of their hearts on the ground,
Grounded in toxicity,
I make wives cry every time their husbands turn to their bottle,
I am one of the factors that lead to domestic abuse,
I claimed over a million lives
In the US in 2021 through overdoses,
So tell me,
How can you stop me by increasing awareness?
Hi, my name is addiction,
Even in the midst of a pandemic,
Opioid addiction has become an epidemic,
So tell me,
How can you slow me down when
I enhance your creativity?

Why would you stop me when
I can make you a high functioning individual?
Count your losses
Give up and give in,
For I have won.

On The Nights That We Don't Make Love

Inspired by the prompt 'on the nights that we don't make love'

On the nights that we don't make love
I still think of you,
I used to speak the hurtful truth
Now I push a pen of positivity
To project hope to the masses,
I looked for you among the heavens but
God told me that you were a hidden angel,
Shining down on me like a ray of light
That was similar to a smile stuck in time
From the poet Arisai,
I was a cynical insomniac
Before I met you,
Yet as our conversations changed
From being pretty to provocative
We became more promiscuous,
Young and gifted,
Yet it was the 'Khemistry' for me
That converted me to

A deep thought lyricist,
I had found it,
The true love that wasn't transient,
So I didn't have to wonder
If you are the one for me while you make
Facial expressions of sudden shock
Like Ms. Jacinda Rodriguez,
Whisper to me all night and
We'll call that an eloquent murmur
A caterpillar,
So as you metamorphose into a butterfly
Captivate my mind with a soft voice
Like Mozeic Insights
On Wednesday nights,
In heels with long flowing black hair
Does that make you an accidental poet?
I sigh, thinking that you are
While this unification of verses is
Making me spit flames like Leon and
Deliver pieces bilingually like if
I'm the monkey king,
I want to give you more but
I only have until 9.30 so that I could see
'Wha gwan' when Ramrock speaks.
On the nights that we don't make love
I still think of you,

Swayed by tequila,
I came from Caroline's creative corner
Citing confessions where I thought
That you were innocent,
Yet if love was a criminal drama,
Then we just starred in a misdemeanour,
A versatile vixen,
So you entice me with an English accent
So that every time I leave
You ensure that I'm back again,
Cognizant of my 'Conshinz'
I stay away from my guilty pleasures
Even if you wear Prada,
Instead I paint you with poetry
While becoming a meticulous wordsmith
Like Ted,
So although I miss you
One day I will see you 'face to face'
Strumming the strings of this acoustic guitar
Like if I'm Peter Coxx with my two Xs.

Write Me A Poem

Inspired by the prompts 'the wolves of worry' and 'these gift-wrapped deaths'

You told me to write you a poem,
So I picked apart pieces of
My prefrontal cortex to produce
A powerful and profound one,
I was a masked poet,
Making misses of melancholy marvel
At this wordplay for you to hear,
Yet you grew tired,
That diagnosis of sickle cell anemia gave
This dark man the blues and although
I was an Archie fan, I was a jughead
That had a hard time choosing between
Betty and a poet named Veronica,
I met many Nicoles, but this fallen angel
Nourished me and told me to
'Just do it' like Nike,
Still I wanted more,
This wolf worried, wondering why
You were wilting away like a flower

That lacked water,
Even though he was winning, he was woeful,
At a crossroads, he looked to his left,
Looking for Adam to whirl words while
He was distracted by a poet in fishnet stockings,
'Your love was a losing game'
So he looked for a 126 area code hoping
To reach Mrs. Carla Jean Stafford
While thinking thoughts by Steve
Caused him to inspire future generations,
In this galaxy of poetry, he hoped
To be an inspiration,
Facing fears of food fortification,
He had the faith to drive, fermenting
Grapes from vines so that you could sip wine,
Trapped by a black widow, he ends his thoughts
Forever trapped in Jan's rhapsody
As he views the rams at dawn.
You told me to write another,
So I pick my pen up,
Telling the truth always so
They call me the righteous poet,
Born to write, I became a lyrically gifted brother,
I have been friends with many Mikes,
But we were never blood brothers,
They told me that the tribe ain't right,

Yet it is still here, and through
This divine epiphany, I was an author
That lyrically reigned, discussing important events
These thoughts of a mature mind
Stopped us from being passively aggressive
So every time I speak out,
They call me black and moody,
They want me to be silent, but
Every time that this poet has spoken,
I show you that I wanted to play clean,
Yet you wanted me to play dirty,
In this poet's playground, penance has
To be paid to the host Frizzy,
An innocent face, but you would get this gifted pen,
These gift- wrapped deaths would be
The end result as you are issued Kheneil
Black's death sentence.

I Hate You

Inspired by the prompt 'Ram it in, twist it, jerk it, done.'

Ram it in!
Dear Covid,
I miss the scent and feel of a woman,
We used to press our bodies together,
So our anatomies became accustomed
To the proximity while we....
Were entranced as we ingested
Each other's essence,
Yet you were lurking,
You ensured that we reiterated and reinforced
The relevant protocols that you rammed
Into our minds
So that we could reflect on the ramifications
Of us being together,
I hate you,
You removed the natural chemistry that
We possessed,
Yet every time that we try to have a civil conversation,
You respond like an uninterested woman

With letters when a man tries
To escape a platonic relation,
So you say:
IHU,
Then you twist it,
Doctors and nurses are our new villains,
They become public relations officers
To advertise a product that was only created recently,
So we don't trust the pros,
Instead we trust the cons,
Not the cons, like if we are evaluating pros and cons
Of a situation, but
The cons that coerce us into conversations
That are laced heavily with controversy,
We kick caution aside,
Enjoying every moment of our lives,
Killing cabin fever in the process,
Your prevalence, although noted is
Not considered, so as the numbers
Increase exponentially,
I can't celebrate birthdays like I used to,
Then you....
Jerk it,
Our minds traverse through brainstorms
While our bodies snap back to reality
While the authoritative figures in society

Perform involuntary actions

Since they are unable to control human behavior,

The knee jerk reaction of a curfew is ineffective,

So you rise,

Surrounded by an army of droplets and ever changing information

Tell me about safety

One mask was enough,

Now we double and triple that sense

Of security unless the digits end with 95,

So I am...

Done,

As a Bajan, I am fed up with this RH,

These extremely hazardous conditions create

Real risks that we try to assess,

Yet our assets dry up,

All I ask is that in 2022,

You return Crop Over to us.

Dear God

Inspired by the prompt 'Flavors of my Pain'

Dear God,
I believe in you, but I have questions,
I am nervous,
So if you see my sweat seeping through
These sebaceous glands,
Then please bear with me,
Why is it that people profess to speak
In your name, yet they gravitate to nepotism?
I have seen delinquents do deadly deeds
That decimated the dreams and desires
Of those who were deemed to be righteous,
So if the meek should inherit the earth,
Then why don't they get the recognition
That they deserve?
We are supposed to be
Under the umbrella of Christianity,
Yet, there is division among denominations
I have seen Anglicans, Methodists and
Adventists close the door
On Jehovah's witnesses,

So if I am to witness the events
That would lead to your second coming
Then could you point me to the credible sources?
You have told me that
I'm blessed and highly favoured but
If all men were truly created equally
Then why did Cain feel compelled to kill Abel?
You have commanded me not to covet but
David sent Uriah to die
So that he could have Bathsheba,
Then he raped her,
Teach me the difference between love and lust
So that I could be a successful servant,
Yet before I do,
Tell me why polygamy causes such controversy now,
Yet Solomon was allowed to have wives,
Mistresses and concubines?
Dear God,
I hope that these questions don't make me
A heathen or a heretic.

Dear God,
I killed alliteration, dragged its corpse up,
Allowed it to be resurrected,
So that we could have a conversation,
I lie between limericks and litanies as

I look over Lamentations,
I was serenaded by sonnets while I speak
Through similes and meticulous metaphors
Whenever I read the book of Psalms,
I hear the haikus of Isaiah, but dear Lord,
I still have questions,
Why is it that in some parts of the world
You are persecuted worse than Stephen
Just because you are a Christian?
Beheaded, not stoned,
They are made martyrs even though
They believed,
Tell me, why is that we sometimes see
So many educated men on the block
Daily with little to no opportunity?
We go after degrees,
Yet still we can't get jobs in that discipline
We go after certificates,
Yet still we hear that we need experience,
I was walking to work one day when
A car stopped, picked up my female coworker and drove off
Even though we were headed
In the same direction,
So tell me, how can we get so passionate
About racism, yet we conveniently choose

To ignore the facets of classism?
Maybe I should also ask humanity but
Thank you for listening
As these burning questions represent
The flavors of my pain.

Mythical

I could tell you tales of
Mythical mermaids and mermen
Who were breathing water but
You would say that I have a vivid imagination,
An allegory that had been attenuated
By alliteration,
Yet all I wanted was a little ration
Of your time,
Those sweet soft kisses were
Still stuck in my mind and as
I try to move on from you,
I realized that I couldn't,
You took my breath away,
Which was funny because a poet
Never gets speechless but
I speak less every time you enter a room,
Damn, my consonants and vowels
No longer make sense,
Yet I still miss the scent of you,
You forced me to die,
Since I could no longer give you compliments,
You supplement me with your essence,

So as I draw my last breath,
While my cells are desiccated due
To a lack of water,
I ask,
May I have my life back?

Pariah

My pen is an attractive amalgamation
Of dutiful dissent, due diligence and omnipotence,
It seeks to reimburse readers of real rhetoric
With writings where we don't alienate human rights,
They had been subjected to fallacies
Where, in order to survive
They fight amongst themselves,
Hoping to be the fittest,
So here I stay, detached from Darwinism,
Yet he thinks that I am naturally selected
To tell... his story,
I puff my chest out,
While my words are delivered bluntly
Like the beak of a Galapagos finch,
I am ready to tell the story of a pariah,
Poetically perched in a position
Where positivity is no longer projected...
From him,
He is lost,
Thrown out from a toxic environment
Where he tried to make it work for his son,
Yet the bills weighed heavily on his heart,

The landlord shared the same gender,
Yet his compassion dimmed
Like a defective 60W bulb that couldn't
Illuminate your kitchen,
So out he went,
Without a job or a home to call his own,
So he searches,
Desperation kicks in,
The measure of a man is no longer applicable,
So he applies for a job to pump gas,
His brother takes him in,
Initially, things seemed to have worked out,
Yet the love for a woman causes them
To part ways,
Now the wounds fester,
She says that she loves him,
Yet, twenty four hours later,
He is out in the cold, with his son,
This is a father's sad tale,
Yet, all they will see is a deadbeat,
It is a small segment of a bigger picture
That we call reality.

Wonderment

I am in wonderment of you,
Inspiring me as your pen strokes
Put me through pericardial effusion,
I love every ounce of you,
Captivate me with your creative concepts
As I become enthused to
Be your only audience,
Tease me with your delivery
So that I could be hypnotized by your voice,
You are my other half,
The voice of reason that forces me
To face my fears and insecurities,
You advocate for women who are
Unable to face the hardships of life,
Let me cry for you,
Since you have been through too much,
Your inner strength calms me
Even though I am strong myself
I adore your head wraps and as I am
Lost in your nakedness,
I wish that I could lie on your chest,
That lovely bosom that nurtures and

Nurses me back to health,
Yet you don't know how talented you are,
But I do,
Your sense of purity is alluring,
Your smile is magical,
Your heart is so big that both of
My hands aren't enough to hold it,
Hear me as I say these three words
That will bind us forever,
I love you.

To Me

If I could place a finger on the point where
My life changed from private to public,
Then it would be the point where
People were preoccupied with whether
Or not you push your penis into a pelvic region
Growth?
Tell me what that is,
Mandela spent 27 years of his life in prison
Yet, we still fight fiercely against segregation
Social status dictates our skewed norms,
Beliefs, norms and values
So the culture created is one where
We are continuously counting casualties
Caused by a disease where we still are
Unable to determine its etiology,
Growth?
Tell me what that is,
I could tell you that I was growing,
Yet, internally the tears were flowing
Every time a man committed suicide because
He was forced to internalize,
I lost a few friends this year:

One to suicide, one to a car accident,
So the images of their faces
Still haunt my memories,
Neither of them reached 35,
So if we are truly talking about growth,
Then direct me to the days
That black men are no longer castigated
For their emotions, or marginalized,
Until then, growth still seems relative
To me.

Time Will Tell

Her world shattered,
So, although she seemed like a sapphire
Shining in sunlight,
Internally, she was drowning in a darkness
A sorrow so grandiose that she could not
Verbalize her true feelings
So time will tell,
Tell me, how can she recover from losing
A firm figure that had been cemented
In her life for over a decade?
'Thirteen years ain't thirteen days' and
As I quote that line, I realized that
It hit different,
He was a good man,
So although she and I were cheering for him,
He didn't make it,
Given a timeline for his demise,
He didn't want her to think about the day
That he would die,
Instead he would smile daily through the pain,
Asking her about her 8 hour day
As if he had no worries,

He wanted her to live her life
Even though he was deteriorating,
I remember when she told me that
She watched as he drew his last breath,
I paused, because even though
I have my own problems,
I listened, knowing that he was
A good man,
Humble, even though his partner
Was a sacred treasure,
I wonder
Why do the good ones die so young?

Time will tell,
These were her words as today comes
To an end and she has to face tomorrow,
Tomorrow:
The day that she bids farewell to her lover,
Her moon, sun and constellations,
Yet she wasn't ready,
Daily, she relives every conversation,
Hoping that through this,
She could feel his presence,
See his smile,
Hear his voice,
Feel his touch,

Yet she can't,
Tomorrow would be the final day
That she would see him physically but
He would live on in her memory,
He could never be replaced,
He was the firm pillar that supported her
When she was weak,
He was her biggest cheerleader,
Waving pom poms so that
She could remember that she could do
Anything,
Now he is gone,
Gone too soon like that old Michael Jackson song
Will she press on?
How will she be tomorrow?
Shopping for clothes today seemed too much,
So when I asked,
'How are you holding up?'
She said
'I don't know Marlo,
Only time will tell.'

About The Author

Marlo Browne is a Barbadian author who has been writing poems since 2009. He self-published his first book **Pictorial: Writing for Stars that want to Return to Constellations** in 2019, in which he envisioned a concept where he could paint pictures with words. Since then, he has taken part in the "16 days of Activism against Domestic Abuse" competition that was held online in November 2020, where he placed third with his poem 'John Keats.' He has participated in both local and international open mics and some of his work has been read by the 'Poetrybattles' and 'The Heart Tribe' communities. In July 2021, he had been the guest on the 'Inside the Chrysalis' podcast, where he featured some of his work from this book. In August of that same year, he published his second book **Marlo Browne presents: The Young and Gifted**, where he takes you down an emotional journey through words. Both books are available on Amazon and have received 5-star reviews.

Since then, he has been interviewed by Danyeil Green of 'Spoken Sol Sessions', Lydia Cook on her Instagram show: 'Beautiful Chaos' and had his own author showcase on the 'Lyrical Reigns Authors', which was hosted by Epiphany Divine. He was one of the featured guests on 'Oh My Word', which he showcased some pieces from his second book in a 20 minute set. He was also one of the features for Nopal Flower's birthday, where he had a thirty minute set, as well as on Jus Stars Inspiring Creativity and Justars Inspiring Poetry where he was the sole poet from Barbados for both of these events and he will be on the latter show again. His poem for the prompt 'On the Nights that We Don't make Love' was also the featured poem on 'The GrapeVine Sway', performed by Miss Tequila Sway herself. Some of his unpublished work was published in 'Poetspeakmagazine' for its November issue as well as the site 'Round Lemon' in the UK.

Manufactured by Amazon.ca
Bolton, ON

35853944R00061